The
Passive Income
Playbook

Raza Imam

WARNING:
This Is NOT a Generic
"Passive Income" Book

Dear reader, I have a confession to make:

When I started this book, I thought I could hire a ghostwriter to write a quick book on making passive income.

What came back was complete crap.

The writer is a great writer.

And I really, really like him.

So this is NOT a comment on his work.

It's actually a comment on my mindset at the time.

I thought I could write something really quickly.

But when I looked at it, I couldn't sell it in good conscience.

It wouldn't help people.

It would tell them something they didn't already know.

It wouldn't inspire them to take action.

As I researched "passive income" on Amazon I saw even crappier books.

Most of them were regurgitating information that you probably already know.

Real estate investing, Investing in stocks, Affiliate marketing.

Blah, blah, blah.

But what they're short on is details.

They lack personal experiences, and stories, and "aha" moments, and breakthroughs, and specific steps, and resources that the author used.

And in my opinion, THAT'S what people need.

So I completely scrapped what my ghostwriter gave me and wrote this entire book from scratch.

I knew that if I released this book, it HAD to be good.

It had to have my personal experiences, it had to document the emotional roller coaster ride I went through on my journey to making passive income. It had to show how I actually overcame my obstacles and eventually succeeded.

Because THAT'S the stuff that motivates people.

Reading a basic "how to" book doesn't help much if it's devoid of stories and personal experiences.

It's not very helpful to know how to generate passive income without knowing what do do when things go wrong.

That's why I'm revealing the exact steps I took to generate passive income.

I share the steps I took.

I reveal the mistakes I made.

You'll learn from my failures so that you don't make the same mistakes I did.

I tell you how I overcame the hurdles, setbacks, and fears I faced.

I explain how I got out of a slump and grew my passive income business when things slowed down.

Because THAT'S what people want to know.

In this book I'm going to give you two things:

1). I'm going to reveal the #1 way to make passive income. Not a list of generic methods that anyone can Google. You'll learn from my failures so you put your efforts on the #1 method to make passive income

2). The step-by-step method I used to generate tens of thousands of dollars of passive income.

I've actually spent thousands of dollars researching, and testing, and learning about this stuff and will share my experiences with you.

I'm pouring my heart and soul into this book.

I'm revealing every trick, secret, resource, and shortcut I know to help you succeed.

Because that's what you need.

That's what I intend to deliver in this short, but powerful book.

But please note: this is no get rich quick scheme.

Building passive income requires a very ACTIVE effort in the beginning.

It's like planting a tree.

You have to choose good quality seeds.

Then locate a fertile plot of land to plant them in.

You then have to water the seed and take care of it as it grows.

Then, once it's mature and starts to bear fruit, you can reap the reward of your work.

If you think you're going to buy this book and make money without any effort, without providing value, and without having to be committed to helping an audience - **please stop reading and put this book down.**

But what I WILL show you is how to fast track the process so you can start making money in as little as 30 days.

Now that that's out of the way… let's begin.

Get Your **Free** _Cheat Sheet_
Of **The Passive Income Playbook**

The Passive Income Playbook is a short read.

I realize that it will take the average person less than an hour to get through the whole thing.

But I believe the strategies contained are so powerful, I want you to know about them, NOW!

So, I want to give you a 4 page "cheat sheet" that covers the main elements in the book.

I show you EXACTLY how to start making $500 to $2500 per month of passive income - in the next 30 days.

When you download the cheat sheet, I'll also send you other exclusive tips, tricks, and secrets to TURBOCHARGE the process and start making passive income - FAST.

Go to NOW For Your FREE Cheat Sheet!

http://www.passiveincomeplaybook.com/

I'll also invite you to join my exclusive "30 Day Challenge" where I help you generate passive income in just 30 days - for FREE.

So Go to NOW For All Your FREE Bonuses!

http://www.passiveincomeplaybook.com/

Table of Contents

Who This Book Is For

The other day I was talking to a good friend of mine about how he has no time for anything.

He has a wife, two kids, a full-time job, and a large extended family that he sees on the weekends.

He's smart, dedicated, and ambitious.

He and I have discussed business for years.

But he feels like he has no time for anything.

Can you relate?

He said he reads about people making passive income online.

But most of them are young college aged kids.

Or single people.

Or people that are about to retire.

Or people that are recently divorced.

The point is that it's HARD to start something up when you have a full-time job, a growing family, and social obligations.

I know EXACTLY how he feels.

I'm 36 years old and a father of 3 young kids aged 10, 7, and 2.

I'm also a husband.

And at the time of me writing this book, I have a full-time job.

But I'm still able to generate $1500 - $2500 per month in passive income.

On autopilot. How?

That's what I'll reveal in this book.

This book is for people like me.

Fathers, mothers, people with jobs that want to make extra money on the side - and eventually double, triple, or even quadruple their income.

It's all possible. I'm doing it now. In this short book, I'll show you how.

Chapter 1: Imagine Yourself Making an Extra $2000/month (in the next 30 days)

What if you could check your phone, at any time of day, and see that you've made money - without actively doing anything?

I'm talking $500 to $2500 per month in the next 30 days..

What if you could do this easily, day in and day out, and keep making more and more money?

What if you could work once, and reap the benefits week after week, month after month?

Sound too good to be true?

It's not.

And I'm going to prove it later in this book.

With real life examples of people that I know.

People like you and me.

Lawyers.

IT professionals.

Busy fathers.

Busy stay at home moms.

Musicians.

People with MBA degrees and six-figure jobs.

College students.

People from other countries like Poland and India.

I'll reveal their names.

How they got started.

And the amazing lives they're living because of the passive income they've earned.

But, I'm getting ahead of myself.

Right now, I want YOU to imagine you're making passive income.

I want YOU to imagine building a business that runs on autopilot.

I want YOU to imagine making thousands and thousands of dollars.

Because before I show you HOW to do it, I need you to believe that it can be done.

I need you to feel the confidence, the motivation, and the desire to make this actually happen for you.

Because once you believe it's possible, you'll take action.

So I want you to just imagine yourself making passive income.

What would your life look like?

How would it feel to be making money, whether it's an extra $500/month, or an extra $5,000 per month?

What would you do with your money?

Would you pay down debt from college, or car loans maybe?

Would you travel to places you've always wanted to visit?

Would you use the extra money to take care of a needy relative?

Or would invest in learning a new talent or skill like a new language, or maybe a musical instrument?

Trust me, the extra money is amazing.

But just imagine what you'd do with the extra time?

What if you got to a point where you could quit your job?

Yes, it'll take consistent effort (all great things do).

But it's possible.

And like I said, I promise to show how other people just like you have done the same thing later in this book.

Just imagine what your life would look like if you didn't have to go to a job.

No more bosses.

No more deadlines.

No more daily commute.

No more fear of being downsized.

But it gets better.

Because building a passive income usually means that you earn money off of a product.

Whether it's book royalties.

Or rental income from property.

Or dividends from shares of a company you own.

Or licenses of software you sell.

Building passive income usually means that you don't have to deal with people.

No selling, pitching, or presenting to clients.

No angry customers.

No hunting investors.

No employees to recruit, hire, or manage.

Just pure profit from a product that sells itself.

That's the beauty of building a passive income.

It's the ultimate form of freedom.

Now there are **TONS** of ways to earn passive income.

And there are lots of books that merely list out all the ways you can earn passive income.

But they are very generic.

And **don't** list detailed steps.

And besides, you probably already know about them.

But in this book, I'm going to reveal the #1 way to build a passive income.

With the exact steps I used to make over $25,000.

It's *fast*.

It's *simple*.

And it requires *minimal* time and money.

Especially when you do it the way I show you.

But here's the thing about passive income…

Unlike actively making money, you have to be patient.

You have to work intelligently.

You have to plan.

But if you do it right, you can go from zero to making thousands and thousands of dollars a month relatively quickly.

And that's exactly what I'm going to show you in this book.

Chapter 2:
Popular Passive Income Strategies (and why I DON'T recommend them for beginners)

There are lots of generic articles, and even books on Amazon that talk about making passive income.

Some of the most popular books are very generic, very high-level, and lack a detailed, step by step plan.

They also go over some of the most common passive income strategies.

But I don't recommend them.

Why?

Because they usually require a large capital investment.

Usually $5,000 or more.

No, that isn't a lot of money in the grand scheme of things.

But it's more than most people want to put down when they're starting off.

My recommendation is to look at this like a business.

Passive income is NOT a game.

It's NOT a scam.

It's a business and it takes work, and planning, and commitment.

That said, there are TONS of passive income activities out there.

But I DON'T recommend them.

Why?

They take too much money.

Or they take too much time.

And if you're a beginner with a full-time job, you probably don't have very much of either one.

So before I go into the best way to make passive income, I want to go over the pros and cons of the most popular methods.

- **Real Estate Investing**: One of the most surefire ways to make money is to invest in real estate (as the old saying goes, invest in land, God is not making anymore). The most common way to invest in real estate is to buy a property, remodel it, and then sell it at a profit. Obviously, there is a high barrier to entry, as even properties in an awful state of disrepair still cost a lot of money. Also, you have to know what you're doing and have lots of time to and money to invest in the upgrade process.

  Verdict: You can make a lot of money, but it takes a LOT of time, money, and expertise to become good at it.

- **Trading Stocks**: Stock trading is another good way of building a passive income, assuming you have some capital to start with. The logic behind trading stocks is not all that different from real estate investing, buy low, sell high. It gets more complicated, and entire books can be written about the topic, so I will not say anymore.

  Verdict: You can make a lot of money, but it takes very specialized knowledge, large amounts of capital, and time to research the market.

- **Blogging**: I've had multiple blogs that made $500 to $1000 per month. So they do work and you can make a good passive income through blogging, it just takes a lot of time and effort.

  Verdict: You can make a good money, especially if you think of it like a business and scale up, build relationships with other bloggers in your niche, write for other blogs in your niche, and invest the time and energy to be a thought-leader. You also have to learn SEO, copywriting, build an email list, and learn to promote with social media. I definitely recommend it, but it's not the best way for beginners to make passive income.

- **E-commerce Store**: E-commerce refers to the process of selling things on Ebay, Shopify, or even on Amazon. E-commerce, much like blogging, requires a lot of time and effort at the beginning. You need to find reliable suppliers, pick a product to sell, create listings, etc. But, once you have the business going, you can sit back and collect your passive income. A well run e-commerce business can generate a lot of money per month; some people even make upwards of $100,000 a year (many make that much per month)

  Verdict: You can make a good money, especially if you sell a hot product. But finding the product is the tricky part. Also, you need to invest considerable amounts of money in paying for ads (Facebook ads are really popular) and split-testing them

- **Membership Sites**: The idea behind membership sites is to create a site that offers great free content, but that also offers great content to premium members. You want to convince visitors to your site that it is worth signing up for a premium membership. This can be done by offering special guides or articles for premium members, or making special functions available to premium members. After that, they pay you monthly to be part of a private group. I'm seeing lots of people create paid membership groups on Facebook around topics like online marketing, fat loss, dating, etc.

  Verdict: This works, but it typically works once you've already established yourself as an expert, be it through your blog, or via a large email list. Membership sites are not recommended for beginners with no audience and no track record.

- **Mobile Apps**: If you are skilled with programming, you can build a good passive income by creating mobile apps. You can either offer ads within the app itself, or create a premium version of the app, and convince people to upgrade. Either way, mobile apps are extremely popular, and you can build quite an impressive passive income off of mobile apps.

  Verdict: Just look at the apps you have downloaded on your phone... someone is making money off of them, so this clearly works. Some people make over $50k/month from their mobile apps. Of course, creating an app is the first issue. Creating an app that people actually want to download is an even bigger issue.

- **Paid Traffic to Affiliate Offers**: Paid traffic is essentially another word for paid ads. So, the idea here is to use paid ads to drive sales to your website, or to a link where the customer can buy whatever product it is that you are selling. If they buy, you get a commission. Sites like Clickbank.com have TONS of affiliate offers in any niche you can think of from relationships, to fitness, to investing, to horse back riding. They mostly have ebooks that sell for $27 to $47. And they offer you a 75% commission if someone buys the book from your link.

  Verdict:This DOES work, but it's getting harder and harder. First, Google and Facebook will penalize you if you buy ads from them and send the traffic straight to the sales page. Second , users don't like it either because you're clearly selling to something to them. This strategy works much better if you build an email list and sell via email after you've built a relationship with your audience. Rather than sending ads straight to a sales page, you send them to your landing page. The landing page offers a free report or video that the user can download by submitting their email address. Over time, you can sell them affiliate products that you recommend - but again - it works way better once you have an actual relationship with them.

- **Photography**: Plenty of sites out there allow you to sell your photos. So, if you are skilled at photography, you can build a great passive income by taking quality "stock" photos. Take generic photos, which would be useful to online business who may be looking for some stock photos to throw on their website.

  Verdict:You'd need to have a great camera and take high-quality pictures. If you're not a photographer already, this is really hard to pull off.

- **Multi-Level Marketing**: I once had a college marketing professor who got his PhD from Harvard. He was a little guy from Texas and had a ton of personality. He used to tell us that if you work hard, you can earn six-figures in 3 years if you work hard with an MLM company. In fact, he did his PhD dissertation on multi-level marketing, so he knew what he was talking about. So yes, some people make a lot of money with MLM. A good friend of mine was making $5000/month from a MLM company. In fact, it was so impressive that he recruited me! Sadly, I didn't make any moneybut I DID learn a lot. If you're good with people, and aggressive at selling, and willing to follow their system and invest time and money in their trainings and events, you can make money.

  Verdict: I really didn't like MLM and was happy to get out. The people who make money in MLM are the ones that follow their system which includes contacting two people per day, inviting friends and family to events, and basically dedicating your life to the organization. On top of that, you make money when you recruit people. So not only do you have to sell their product (which in most cases is really good), you have to convince other people to start selling the product too. And that just wasn't for me.

So again, people DO make money this way.

And I know people that are making money from all of these methods.

But they take quite a bit of specialized knowledge, or time, or a significant investment.

That's why I don't think they're the best way for beginners to make passive income.

You should definitely branch out into these - and I may even write a book on how I've used some of these methods to make money in the future.

But my goal here is to help you start making your first $100 passively.

Because once you do, you'll be hooked.

And you'll have the belief and self-confidence to keep doing it over and over again so that your first $100 turns into $1000 and then $10,000 and beyond.

The good news is that once you do master this, you can use the methods I mentioned above.

But my goal is to make you passive income - FAST so that you can scale it up and then diversify.

Chapter 3: The Emotional Roller Coaster Ride That (finally) Led Me to Making $25,000 in Passive Income

In this book, I'm going to show you the FASTEST way to get started making a passive income.

And believe me, I've tried a LOT of methods.

I got recruited into an MLM company when I was in my early 20's because a friend of mine was making $5,000 per month passively.

Sadly, I made nothing.

Then I got into real estate investing.

I read and read and read about it.

But unfortunately I didn't have any money to put into it.

So again, I didn't make anything.

Then I got into online marketing by taking a free program called "The 30 Day Challenge" by an Australian marketer named Ed Dale.

The premise of the course was to help people make their first dollar online by the end of the free 30 day program.

And it started to work.

I made a site about the Palm Pre cell phone for testing purposes.

And though that site didn't make any money, I learned how to buy a domain name, setup web hosting, install Wordpress, create content, and do onsite and offsite search engine optimization.

After learning the process on that site, I created another site about isometric exercises.

I called it IsometricExerciseSite.com

And within a few weeks, it started ranking highly in Google for terms like "isometric exercises" and "plyometric exercises" along with a bunch of other related terms.

I was getting like 150-500 visitors to that site per month.

Passively.

Then I put a link in the sidebar recommending a fitness ebook.

If someone clicked that link and bought the fitness ebook, I would get a 60% commission.

I still remember my first sale.

And it was an awesome feeling.

I couldn't believe that I was actually making money online.

I remember making my first $100 online in 2009. I was shocked. I couldn't believe that I've actually made money online.

I got addicted to it.

Over the next few months, I kept making more and more money until I started making $500/month consistently.

It was such a liberating feeling.

But then, Google made some changes and I lost my website rankings.

And when I lost my search rankings in Google, my income completely tanked.

Back to the drawing board...

But since I had learned about SEO, I decided to offer SEO services to local businesses in Chicago.

So I found someone on Craigslist that had a website about the raw food diet.

He needed me to do his SEO so that he could get high rankings and sell ebooks from his site.

Unfortunately that never worked out.

I wasn't able to manage his expectations and failed to deliver what he was asking of me.

So then, I decided to focus on my own site again.

I had seen that lots of people search for coffee makers online, so I decided to create a website to sell coffee makers.

So I got to work.

After about 6 months I was able to rank my site (TheCoffeeMakerStore.com) on the first page of Google for the word "coffee makers" and a bunch of other terms.

The only problem is that I was dropshipping - meaning I didn't own the inventory.

I was simply using pictures and descriptions on my website, and then when someone bought, I would purchase the coffee maker from the supplier and have them deliver it to the customer.

Although I was able to market the website and get decent traffic to it, I completely failed at actually delivering the coffee makers because the warehouse often times didn't even have the inventory that I was displaying on my website.

What a hassle!

Not to mention the headaches of dealing with credit card processing.

Needless to say, despite me marketing the site really well, it never made any money.

So then I decided to start doing video marketing and ranking YouTube videos high in YouTube and Google.

The YouTube videos were fitness related and simply linked to a fitness ebook that was a competitor to P90X.

Now this was really good, and I ended up making hundreds and hundreds of dollars a month.

This is a great strategy and I highly recommend it, but you have to be comfortable on camera.

Then, after a few months, YouTube changed their algorithm, and I lost all of my traffic from YouTube.

Once again, my income tanked.

So then I decided to create yet ANOTHER fitness website.

I used my SEO skills to get it to rank in Google and within a few months, I was making $500/month again.

All was good.

Until it wasn't.

See, Google made two big algorithm updates that caused my sites to go down in the rankings again.

And once again, my passive income vanished.

At this point I hit a crossroads.

I had been burned by Google twice and by YouTube once.

So then I was contacted by a guy that told me I should write my OWN book and sell it on my own website.

He had done the same and had made thousands of dollars per month.

He helped me come up with the hook and title of the book.

I called it *"The Science of Getting Ripped"*.

I liked the idea so I paid him $800 to help me write the sales letter for the book.

So to write the book, I created an outline with bullet points, and then I literally dictated my book using an app called Rev.com

You download their app, record your voice, and then upload it to them so they transcribe your voice into text.

Best of all they only charged $1 per minute and transcribe it within 24 hours.

So I was able to write my book that way within about 2 months.

By the time I was ready to sell, I launched it to my email list.

My email list was about 2500 people at the time.

When I launched it, I made about $1000.

Now it was a great feeling, but I didn't make much more than that.

Then someone told me to try Facebook ads.

So I set up Facebook ads to point to my website.

The goal was to have people from Facebook come to my site and buy my book.

Sadly, it never worked.

I spent hundreds of dollars getting people to my site.

Then, I got my Facebook ads account banned because they are very strict with fitness related offers, and apparently I broke one of their rules related to the images I was using in my ads.

If you know anything about Facebook, once they ban you from advertising on their site, it's final.

So there I was, with a book that I had spend over $1000 to create and market.

But I barely broke even.

I was so frustrated because I thought this was going to be it.

I thought my book would sell and I'd be making tons of passive income again.

But I didn't.

So I gave up for a while.

But then, I read a blog post by a guy named David that renewed my hope again.

He had been making money writing and selling fitness books on Amazon Kindle.

I had heard about Amazon Kindle publishing before, but I didn't have the time or energy to think about it.

But now I was intrigued.

He even had a Kindle book called "*Write Book, Make Money*" where he explained his entire process.

I read and reread it.

I put myself in his shoes.

I imagined I was him.

Then I started taking the steps he laid out in the book.

It took me a few weeks to format my book for Kindle.

I could have paid someone on Fiverr to do it, but since it was my first time, I wanted to do it myself.

After that, I launched my book for 99 cents.

First to my email list.

It sold over 100 copies.

"Awesome" I thought to myself.

Amazon only offers a 35% royalty for books that are sold for less than $2.99, so I only made $35 from that promotion to my email list.

But that's ok because those initial sales helped me climb up in the rankings within my categories.

Then I scheduled a bunch of promotions on websites that promote Kindle books.

I'll reveal those sites later in this book, but I staggered them, one day at a time.

By the end of that week, I was a bestseller in multiple categories.

You can see in the screenshot below:

I was so excited!

I was making 15-20 sales per day.

That's when I decided to increase my price to $1.99.

Then to $2.99.

At that point I was eligible to receive 70% royalties on my book.

It kept selling and selling and selling despite the price increase.

So then I increased it to $3.99 and eventually up to $4.99.

It was an AMAZING feeling to be making nearly $2,000 per month from this book.

A book that I had worked so hard on.

And it was pure passive income.

A few months after, I released a paperback version of the book, which I sell for $19.99.

I was hooked to the process, and from that point on, I was DETERMINED to scale this up and write more books and increase my passive income.

So that's my crazy, emotional roller coaster of a story on the way to making passive income.

The beauty of this is that once you sell one book, not only can you replicate the process for other books, you can build a backend business.

I'm talking video courses, mastermind groups, coaching, seminars, and live events.

This is how millionaires are born.

And it ALL starts from one book.

But let's not get ahead of ourselves.

I want to walk you through the process in this book.

So, if you're looking for the easiest, fastest, most reliable way to make a passive income, I would have to say that there's been nothing nearly as effective as writing a book and publishing it on Amazon Kindle.

Publishing on Kindle allows you to make money very fast and does NOT require you to know anything about email marketing, web hosting, Wordpress setup, split-testing, SEO, or conversion optimization.

That's all good to know, but it's pretty advanced and beyond the reach of most beginners.

The first thing I'm going to tell you is that if you have not written an ebook, the most important thing to do is just to get the book out there.

Chapter 4: Why Kindle Books Are the EASIEST Way to Make Passive Income

World renowned copywriter Gary Halbert once asked his students:

"If you and I both owned a hamburger stand and we were in a contest to see who would sell the most hamburgers, what advantages would you most like to have on your side?"

The answers varied.

Some said they wanted the advantage of better meat to make better tasting hamburgers.

Others said they wanted sesame seed buns.

Others said they wanted a better location.

Others said they'd offer lower prices. Etc.

After all of his students finished giving their answers, he said,

"O.K., I'll give you every single advantage you asked for. I, myself, only want one advantage and, if you will give it to me, I will whip the pants off of all of you when it comes to selling burgers!"

"What advantage do you want?" they asked him.

"The only advantage I want," he said *"is A STARVING CROWD!"*

That right there summarizes why Kindle publishing so such a great opportunity.

You have a built-in market that goes there to BUY.

I've had a business before.

And I know how hard it is to get new customers.

In fact my crazy-Texan-Harvard-PhD marketing professor in college said it's 3 to 5 to 7 times harder to get a new customer than to sell to an existing one.

In college I started a software development company with a friend.

It ended up making $30k/month.

Which was great.

What was not so great is the amount of time it took to actually do the work.

And the fact that we had to hire employees overseas.

At the end of the day, I was bringing home $2k per month.

We were making $360,000 in revenue and I was making about $25,000 in take home pay.

It's embarrassing even saying that.

But I was young and it was a great learning lesson.

Eventually we went out of business when the economy tanked in 2008.

But, that's a story for another day.

Like I mentioned earlier, I started making money from a fitness blog and was thrilled.

I still remember my first sale.

I couldn't believe it.

But it did take some time to think about a niche that I wanted to create a site about.

I knew I liked fitness, and wanted to create a niche fitness concept, so I wrote about isometric exercises.

Then I had to create the site.

And buy a domain name.

And setup web hosting.

And learn about installing Wordpress.

Then I had to create write the articles and create content that would appeal to my audience.

That meant I needed to research keywords.

And analyze the search engine results pages for the keywords that I wanted to rank for.

So I had to learn the different keyword tools.

Then once my site was up and had content on it, I had to learn about ranking it so that people found it on Google.

And that was a whole nother process.

Imagine This...

What if there was a website with 300 million monthly visitors.

Unlike Google where people go to search for information.

Or YouTube where people go to watch entertaining videos.

Or Facebook where they go to share videos and pictures with their friends.

Or Linkedin where they go to look for a job.

What if they came to this website to **BUY**?

What if they stored their credit card with this website?

What if they were so eager to spend their money on this website that they could literally click one button and instantly have what they want?

Wouldn't you want to figure out how to sell your stuff there?

Well that's exactly why publishing on Amazon Kindle is so popular.

Because people on Amazon are there to spend money.

All you have to do is understand what they want - and give it to them!

The amazing news, is that out of all of the ebook publishing platforms like Nook, Kobo, and iBooks, Amazon Kindle has roughly 75% market share.

So they're literally the juggernaut in the industry.

That's why I truly believe that Kindle publishing is the best, fastest, most reliable way for beginners to start making money online.

And publishing it on Kindle makes it so incredibly easy.

Because you can focus on blogging and podcasting later, but writing a book is what makes all of that much, much easier.

Speaking from experience, Amazon Kindle is the way to make passive income, it's because I've tried a lot of different methods.

You don't have to market very hard because there's already a built-in market!

And you know what they're buying.

How cool is that?

You don't have to create something and hope that someone buys.

You can literally see what's already selling, read the negative reviews, and then create an even better book.

I just gave away a very valuable secret right there.

Go where the market already is.

Go where they're spending money.

Research what they're spending money on.

And most importantly, research what they love and hate about it.

Because if you can do this, you'll get inside the heads of your customer, you'll understand what the problems they're facing, and you'll understand their deepest desires.

Armed with that knowledge, you can quickly create a book that taps into those emotions and almost forces them to buy from you.

Not because of any sneaky tricks or sleazy sales tactics, but because you took the time to understand your audience and give them what they want.

That's why publishing on Amazon is an amazing way to generate passive income.

Publishing a book on Amazon Kindle is way easier than starting a blog, creating content, marketing that content, getting high rankings in the search engines, and eventually, hopefully, making a sale from either your own product or an affiliate product.

That's why I say out of all the methods that you could use, writing a book on Amazon Kindle is the easiest way because at the end of the day, if you know enough about a certain topic, whether it's weight loss, or parenting, or cooking, or whatever you're interested in, you can write a book about it.

And it doesn't need to be a 300 page, 150,000 word book.

In fact, some of the most successful books on Amazon Kindle are between 10,000 and 20,000 words.

Using the techniques I reveal later in this book, you can do that in as little as 7 days - assuming you're committed and ruthless with your time.

If you can do that in Microsoft Word or in a word processor document, all you really have to do is do a little bit of basic formatting, submit it to Kindle, put it in the right categories, and then promote it.

That's really the way to get your Amazon Kindle book out there in the market so you can start making money from it.

Add that to the fact that Amazon.com is probably the world's most trusted e-commerce site, they have hundreds of millions of people's credit cards on file.

Most people on Amazon, after they read a couple positive reviews, they just hit that buy now button, or that 1 click buy button.

There's a very low amount of friction, meaning it's not very hard to sell something on Kindle if you have good reviews and a compelling description of your product.

That's why it's so important to understand your market.

Because once you do, you can tailor your title, subtitle, description, and cover to address the needs, wants, and desires of your market.

Then the book basically sells itself.

Also, another interesting statistic is Amazon is selling so many Kindle books that digital books and ebooks are being sold way more than physical, paperback and hardcover books.

So the market is only growing.

And Amazon knows this.

They're making it really easy for authors to write and publish and market books, but at the same time, it's a really good opportunity and the timing is really critical for you right now.

That's because there are a lot of low quality books entering the market.

What's going to happen, I predict in the next 6 to 12 months, Amazon will likely become more stringent in the type of books that they allow people to write.

This is really why it's your opportunity to write a good quality book and publish it on Amazon Kindle, so that you can really start making passive income.

If you already have a book or an idea written, or an idea for a book that at you plan on writing, that's great, but if you don't that's okay.

Just keep reading, because I'm going to prove that you're already an expert.

I'm going to show you how to come up with ideas for a book if you don't have one right now.

I'll also show you how to get the book written really fast.

Because I'll tell you, writing the book and completing it is the easy part.

It's actually marketing it, promoting it, and making money from it that most people don't know how to do, but that's okay because you're in the right spot and I'm going to show you exactly how to do that.

Let me assure you, once you start doing well, passive income becomes a very active endeavor.

Because you want to keep doing more and more of it so you make more and more money.

At some point, you'll start making more money than you do at your job.

And that's when things get really fun.

But as much fun as passive income is, understand that a majority of your time will be spent marketing.

And I'm not talking about promoting.

Yes, I'll show you where to promote your book and how specifically advertise it so it makes the most money.

But promoting your book won't help you sell it unless you understand your target audience.

It's kind of like going into a swanky five-star restaurant with an internationally renowned chef in the most expensive part of town and yelling:

"Hey everyone, McDonald's is selling Big Macs for 99 cents!"

Will you make a scene?

Yes.

Will everyone notice you?

Yes.

Will anyone even think of getting up and following your crazy butt to the nearest McDonald's?

I'll let you answer that.

That's why I tell people that marketing does NOT only mean promoting.

It means understanding the needs of your market, digging down to research their deepest desires and most intimate emotions.

It means looking at the topics, titles, subtitles, descriptions, and covers of bestselling books.

Because the only way to make real money in any business is to understand what your market is looking for - and then give it to them.

And Amazon makes that SO incredibly easy, you can literally understand your market by reading reviews and immediately create something that they want.

And after you become successful selling books on Amazon Kindle, you can start building a website, create a course, or launch a membership site online that allows you to scale up your income.

That's how you build a long-term business that can make hundreds of thousands of dollars per year.

Just imagine the opportunities you could have from writing a bestselling book.

Imagine getting invited to popular podcasts, and being interviewed by popular bloggers, and even being featured in the media.

Imagine people reading your book and then contacting your for coaching, or mentorship, or for consulting.

That's the power of writing a bestselling book.

Chapter 5: You ALREADY Are An Expert (and I can prove it)

Writing a book is hard.

Or is it?

I want you to think about that for a second.

Because even though I don't personally know you, I think you have a book in you.

Doubt me?

Well consider this…

Writing a book isn't as hard as you might think.

And if you've been alive for longer than 15 years, you probably have enough expertise in *something* to show others how to do it.

I'll go into examples below, but consider this.

Most non-fiction books revolve around solving some kind of problem, or helping people get to some kind of desired state.

The classic adage is that if you talk about health, wealth, or relationships, you'll never go broke.

That's why diet and weight loss books, magazines, pills, potions, gadgets, surgeries, and articles sell so well.

To the tune of billions of dollars per year.

Because people have a visceral desire to look and feel better.

It's the same reason why people that talk about real estate investing, investing stocks, social media marketing, SEO, sales, how to create business plans, etc. do so well.

They are teaching people how to make more money and become more wealthy.

And that stuff sells.

So like I said, you ARE an expert in something.

And if you can spin your expertise and link it to health, wealth, or relationships, you're golden.

I'll show you want I mean later in this chapter.

Keep in mind, you don't need to be a professional.

For example, I'm not a bodybuilder, or a certified personal trainer, or a health coach.

But I did write a bestselling fitness book.

Why?

Because I'm a normal guy and I was still able to get in shape despite a busy job, a growing family, and a long daily commute.

Rather than being viewed as an "impostor", I was viewed as someone who was able to "figure it out".

And if you look at the reviews from my book "The Science of Getting Ripped", you'll see that it's helped a lot of people.

So stop thinking you're an impostor, or a fake, or not worthy to write.

If you've solved a specific problem, then you ARE qualified to write.

And people will be willing to pay you to learn how you did it.

So be sure to include your personal story.

Share your struggles.

Share your breakthroughs and "aha" moments.

Share the resources you used to achieve your goal and get the results you got.

Because THAT'S what people want to know.

Like the popular phrase goes "*facts tell, stories sell*".

But as far as you being an expert, think about the following list of topics because I'm sure you know quite a bit about at least ONE of these topics.

Remember, you don't need to be an "expert".

You DO need to either have real life experience solving a real problem that people face OR you should interview experts that have done something and compile *their* stories and put it in a book.

That's what an unknown author named Napolean Hill did in 1937.

He interviewed the multi-millionaire businessmen of his time and distilled their advice into easy to digest points and called it "Think and Grow Rich".

As you may know, the book has been a bestseller for the past 81 years.

So the key is to focus on a problem or question that your potential readers could have, and to solve that problem or answer that question in the form of an e-book, either with your own experience, or with someone else's.

But remember, it has to be a real problem that people care about and are willing to spend money on.

If you don't solve a real need, then you likely won't make much income.

If you're already in a high-skilled field like real estate, law, medicine, accounting, computer programming, project management, human resources, copywriting, public speaking, finance, architecture, sales, human resources, organizational change, online marketing, social media expert, or any other highly skilled field, you're GOLDEN.

You have the technical knowledge and experience that you can easily monetize via a book.

Like I've said before, you have to sell your story.

Your personal experiences.

How you overcame your struggles.

Because that's what people buy.

But what if you don't have a professional background?

No problem.

Bestselling author Hal Elrod wrote a book called "*The Miracle Morning Routine*" after getting in a car accident.

And he's built a multi-million dollar business from it.

Amazing, right?

So you don't need to be an expert in a profession.

You just need to have a great story to tell that solves a problem.

Here are a few examples:

- **House training a puppy**: Puppies are often bought on a whim. Someone is walking buy a pet store, or sees an bad from a breeder, and suddenly they just have to have the cute little puppy. This often leads to people having pets that they are not ready to care for properly. These people get frazzled very easily and tend to go looking for house training tips and strategies online. Now, I know what you are thinking, "I can't write a book about house training a puppy. I'm not a professional dog trainer." But the truth is that if you've successfully trained a dog before, or better yet, grew up around dogs, then you can write a very good ebook about house training a puppy. Personal experience counts for a lot. Your readers want to know about your struggles of coming home to a mess on the carpet. They want to hear how you solved that problem if you recommend a certain training strategy or tip, then follow it up with a quick story about what happened when you tried it on your own dog.

- **Getting in Shape**: Everyone wants to get in shape at some point in their life. Sure, there are popular weight loss programs and fitness routines, but do you know why they sell? Because of the results they achieve. In other words, the before and after transformation pictures is what convinces people to buy those programs. So if you've gotten in shape, and you have before and after pics, you can simply write a book documenting how you did it, what you ate, how long it took, and what you felt during the process. And believe me, people will buy it because you're a real person just like them.

- **How to Put a Baby to Sleep**: When we had our first child, getting him to go and stay asleep was so hard. We expected that in the beginning. But not six months into it. So out of desperation, my wife bought 3 books on Amazon about putting a baby to sleep. She read about the different methods and philosophies. She even hired a baby sleep consultant after reading one of her books that she bought from Amazon. We now have 3 kids so my wife has a ton of experience. I joke that if my wife wanted to, she could write her own book on the subject - and people would buy it.

- **Solving a Specific Health Issue** (acne, back pain, etc.): I used to have weird shoulder pain due a weight lifting injury. So I started looking for remedies on YouTube and Google. Luckily it was a minor issue and the advice I learned in a few YouTube videos solved the problem, but if it was a more complicated issue, I would have bought a book about it. Just to be clear, I'm not talking about writing a guide on how to cure cancer or deal with life threatening injuries; but rather health issues like acne, back pain, neck pain, stuffy noses, etc. Health issues like that can usually be managed through home remedies, and thus many people do not go to the doctor for them. This is where your ebook comes in. Lots of people have solutions or tips for dealing with managing chronic pains, bad cases of acne, and clogged nasal passages (just to name a few health issues); usually because they themselves have dealt with these issues before. So, if you have some home remedies, passed down through your family for generations, that helps deal with acne, then you can compile them into an ebook. You can include strategies for reducing acne and managing acne in addition to your own home remedies. The same goes for chronic pain; everyone has their own stretches, exercises, etc., that they use to help remedy chronic back and neck pain; someone who is currently suffering from chronic pain would most likely love to learn about them in an easy to read ebook.

- **Using a Specific Social Media Platform to Grow Your Business**: Now here's a real money maker, especially if you sell to the right audience. Imagine you're a small business person with a struggling floral shop. You've tried different ways to advertise and none of them has really worked for you. You know about Instagram, and Facebook, and Twitter, and Snapchat, but you don't know how to use them to promote your business. What if someone wrote a book showing you exactly how to use those platforms to grow your business. What if they included screenshots, and detailed explanations, and results of other businesses like you that used these platforms to grow their business. Wouldn't you buy it? Of course you would! And people ARE making money writing about using LinkedIn, Facebook, Instagram, and SnapChat, so if you know how to use these platforms to grow a business, you can too.

- **Dealing with Stress**: Chronic stress is a public health issue. It is the root cause of so many diseases and disorders that there is a billion dollar industry around stress relief, from books to expensive seminars. If you've discovered how to conquer stress and tension in your life, then people want to know. It's even better if you have a high-stress life like being a busy parent, or a business owner, or a corporate executive, or a grief counselor. Your advice will ring true because of your background and struggles. If you have personal experience dealing with stress, and have developed a unique way of dealing with it, then compile your expertise into an ebook. Because if your story resonates with your audience, the book will sell quite well.

- **Creating a Business Plan That Generates Money**: It may sound odd, but you would be surprised by the amount of people who rush into a business without having a clear, concise idea of what they want their business to accomplish in the next few years. If you have experience running or creating a small business, then you can write a very good ebook detailing how to create a clear business plan. Obviously, this ebook would not be targeted at high level CEOs, but at small business owners. So be to tailor the book to the specific field you have experience with. Have you started a floral shop? Are you a dentist that has grown your practice? Are you a marketing expert that has shown small businesses how to grow? If so, document it.

- **Photography Tips**: If you have ever bought a camera for someone as a present before, then you know that buying someone a quality camera almost instantly turns them into an amateur photographer for a couple weeks. Most people eventually settle down and only use the camera for special occasions, but some others develop an actual passion for photography. My former boss was obsessed with his camera, always reading about it, researching it, and taking photos during his family vacation. If you're like him, you could easily write a book about photography for beginners. Since schooling or workshops hosted by professionals can be expensive, would be amateur photographers will often search online for helpful EBooks, guides, blogs, etc. A quality ebook written by someone with experience in amateur photography can focus on a wide array of topics; including what accessories to get, how to properly photograph landscapes and people, how to set up a shot, the topics are endless.

- **Wedding Planning**: Expecting parents are some of the most stressed people in the world, but brides and grooms to-be aren't far behind. I know I was stressed when I planned my wedding! Since most people do not know the first thing about wedding planning, they will inevitably turn to the internet for information, inspiration, and ideas. If you have experience planning weddings, then making a clear, easy to follow EBook detailing how to properly plan for a wedding (as well as detailing tips and tricks for how to get the best deals, save money, etc.) would be a great idea. Not only will it sell well, but because people are always getting married, you'll never have to worry that your book becoming obsolete.

- **How to Better at Public Speaking**: Not everyone is born to speak to crowds, but unfortunately for those people, giving speeches to an audience is a talent that is quite helpful in many different business sectors. Given how important public speaking is, many people will turn to the internet to learn how to do it properly. If you consider yourself a natural speaker, or you overcame poor public speaking skills, then you have the ability to write a bestselling book. Give people exercises that they can do in front of family to improve their speaking skills, give them tips to help get their nerves under control while speaking, etc.

- **Mentoring Troubled Youth**: I recently heard that "school refusal" is becoming a thing with teenagers. They aren't quite dropping out, but they're refusing to go to school due to a variety of reasons (bullying, anxiety, substance abuse, etc.) Then there's the issue of kids with domestic problems that affect their performance and behavior in school. Lastly, there's the issue of kids that just don't apply themselves academically. Mentoring troubled youth probably has some of the greatest social impact on society. Mentoring troubled youth, putting them on the right path, and actually connecting with them is a very high-yield activity for society. And any stories, techniques, or results you can share would likely do very well. Just imagine writing a book on how to prevent bullying, a little book you write could turn into major media coverage if the book really produces results, or shares your "in the trenches" story of how you solved it at your school.

- **Building Money-Making Websites**: Remember how I talked about social media ebooks and how they can be useful for businesses and marketers who need to use social media, but don't know how? Well, the same principle applies for website building. Plenty of small business owners and internet marketers need to create websites. Often times the technical part isn't hard, it's the messaging. Writing the copy. Creating "words that sell". That speak to a certain market. That address a major problem. That promise an end result. So even if you aren't technical, if you know how to write, you can STILL show people how to make money with their website.

- **Selling Products Online:** There are a LOT of people making a full-time income selling products on EBay, Amazon, Craigslist, etc. For others, it's a nice source of income on the side. Either way, more and more people are starting to experiment with selling products online. Because of that, online courses and ebooks detailing how to get into selling online are very popular. It is not surprising, the process may seem simple, but actually getting into selling online is very complicated. You have to know the rules of the site you are selling on, you have to know what type of products sell best, and you have to know where to get products at cheap prices. If you have ever sold products online successfully, then compiling your experiences and knowledge into a book is really a no brainer. There are always new people getting into online retail for the first time, and they are always looking for guides, courses, and ebooks to help them out.

- **Saving Money and Personal Finance**: Not everyone is great when it comes to managing their money. Some people cannot seem to live within their means, and spend money like it never runs out. If you have any tips or strategies for saving money and budgeting properly, then putting them into an book is a greatidea. You don't even need to say anything new or novel. You can simply share your experiences with using the "envelope system" like Dave Ramsey talks about. Or you could write about how you went for 6 months without eating out. Or how you got out of debt in 12 months by selling unwanted stuff in your house. I know people that have done stuff like that and their stories are really, really interesting. If they compiled it into a book I'd definitely want to buy it.

- **Grooming/Beauty/Personal Care**: Do you know about men's grooming? Or looking good in your 40's? Or do you have an eclectic sense of style by shopping solely at thrift stores? If so, I'm willing to bet that people will pay for it. Looking good and being accepted are basic human emotions, and if you tap into that, you can start to build a very nice passive income. You don't have to work at a beauty salon or be a professional stylist to write a book about personal grooming. If you feel you have a good sense of style, or your friends and family are constantly complimenting your grooming, then you can write a quality book about the topic.

- **Travel Advice**: Let's say you were (or currently are) a backpacker, travelling around the world, staying in hostels and Airbnbs in exotic countries. What if you finance your travels from credit card airline points? Don't you think people would want to know about that? What if you compiled a list of the best hotels, best credit cards, and best restaurants you've discovered in your years of travelling. Wouldn't people want to buy that? Or let's say you're a corporate road warrior, travelling 5 days a week and you've figured out how to stay in shape while on the road. Don't you think people similar to you would want to know that knowledge?

This list barely scratches the surface of what you could write about.

But you can probably see that the most popular topics address a core human emotion.

Whether that's the emotion to make more money.

Or the emotion to be liked and loved and desired by other people.

Or the emotion of being freedom and peace of mind.

You already ARE an expert in something.

Even if you don't think you are, your life experiences and unique perspective gives you credibility.

Your job is to figure out how to link your expertise to a basic emotion.

I can't stress that enough.

So if you can tie your topic into health, wealth, or relationships, you'll be golden.

So if you write about gardening, you could write about how to create a stunning backyard that boosts your property value by $25,000.

Or if you write a cookbook, you can focus on how your recipes save money, or help lose weight, or can save a busy family precious time because they're so quick and easy to cook.

Or what if you're a swim instructor and have built a side business teaching kids how to swim on the weekends. You could write a book showing how you've helped mentor kids through swimming, and share the life lessons you've learned. Or you could explain how you've built a profitable side hustle by teaching kids how to swim.

So spend some time thinking about what you're good at and what you want to share.

Because as long as you know how to relate that to core human emotions and desires, you can make a very sustainable passive income.

Chapter 6: Real People That Are Actually Doing It - Why Can't You?

So far in this book I've revealed the best way for beginners to earn passive income.

I've explained how to scale it up.

I've given you examples of things that you could write about.

I've also shown you how to take virtually any topic and

Now that I've showed you that you're an expert, I want to show you other people that have built great passive incomes by showcasing their expertise.

Keep in mind, these are real people.

Just like you and me.

They've worked hard and put their heart and souls into creating something of value for their audience.

I know these people.

I've read their books.

I've spoken to them.

And I can tell you that they're regular people.

The only difference is that they've learned how to take their knowledge and build a passive income business.

And I want to share their stories so that you have the belief and self-confidence to do the same. ow you how to do the same.

Steve Scott: Steve Scott is the self-publishing godfather. He's made approximately $500,000 from his books on Kindle over the past 2 years.

He writes about business and authorship, but has recently struck gold by writing about productivity habits.

He then expanded that into a whole line of books about mindfulness and digital declutter.

His books are routinely in the top 100 on Amazon and he even had the #1 best selling on Amazon at one point.

But the lesson to be learned is that he had to start somewhere.

As a self-published author, he had to write, publish, and market his books by himself.

I remember him writing as far back as 2013.

He just wrote and wrote and wrote.

If you look at his earlier books, the topics were a little scattered and the book covers were a bit less "crisp" than they are now.

But he kept at it, and kept getting better and better.

He now has between 40 and 50 published books.

He can put out a book and instantly make it a bestseller because he has such a huge following.

But that doesn't mean he's writing 100,000 word opuses.

His books are between 10,000 and 20,000 words.

If you write 2,000 words per day, which is roughly two single-spaced pages in Microsoft Word, you could do that in a week.

Take a look at some of his books on Amazon for inspiration.

Barrie Davenport: Barrie Davenport is another bestselling author, and is a partner of Steve Scott.

She writes about personal development, self confidence, and mindfulness and has recently co-authored books with Steve Scott.

Take a look at some of her books on Amazon to see what kinds of books sell well.

Michal Stawicki: Michal Stawicki is a lot like me - except that he lives in Poland and I live in Chicago.

He has two sons and a daughter and an IT background.

He also got started as a self-published author, writing about fitness and personal development.

He's a down-to-earth, straight-talking, no nonsense kind of guy that has earned a nice side income writing books.

In his books, he shares personal stories, real life examples, and detailed techniques and methods he's used to improve his life.

Some of his most popular books are *"The Art of Persistence"* and *"Know Yourself Like Your Success Depends On It"*

Zoe McKey: Zoe McKey has an amazing story.

She's been living on her own and taking care of herself since the age of 14.

She had to build self-confidence and emotional intelligence quickly so that she could make it in the world.

She is upbeat, kind, and very hardworking - largely due to her situation.

Now in her 20's she's a world-travelling, multi-bestselling author, and communication coach.

She writes about personal development topics such as emotional intelligence, boosting confidence, and conquering fear.

She puts out a book almost every month (or so it seems) and she routinely gets amazing reviews and tons of sales.

Her work ethic is what I admire so much.

Her bestselling books are *"Daily Habit Makeover"*, *"The Critical Mind"*, and *"Tame Your Emotions"*, and *"Find What You Were Born For"*.

Patrick King: If Steve Scott is the self-publishing godfather, Patrick King is a close runner up.

This former lawyer turned author has a very unique background.

He started off writing dating profiles for guys online.

You know, sites like Match.com, OKCupid, PlentyofFish, etc.

He knew how to write profiles that would get women interested in his clients.

He transitioned out of that business (maybe because he found those guys to be a bit sleazy) and used his communication skills to write bestselling communications books.

In one interview he did, he was quoted as making $14,000 per month from his books.

It's a staggering figure, but he's earned it.

Patrick's experience as a lawyer taught him the importance of just grinding out the work.

Like other authors mentioned, he routinely puts out a book a month.

In fact, in one interview, he said he wrote 20 books his first year.

How is that possible?

Well, I'll share one strategy later in this book.

But that's another key to success.

Consistency.

Like other authors, he's written, and written, and written.

I'm not saying you have to write dozens of books.

I AM saying that you can learn from his progression as an author.

You'll see how he kept getting better and better.

So if you don't feel like you're up to snuff, you'll get there if you work hard enough.

Some of his bestselling books are "*Conversation Tactics*", "*Fearless Social Confidence*", and "*Magnetic Charisma*".

Som Bathla: Som is a great new author from India.

He's routinely putting out a book a month as well and writes about personal development topics like improving focus, productivity, and mindfulness.

I don't know how long he's been writing, but what I love is that he and his wife work on this books together.

He writes, and she helps create the covers and edit (from what I recall).

What I also like about Som is that he's a regular guy that decided to take action.

When he first got started, he reached out to a few authors and asked them for advice.

That was a bold move that took courage, but it was totally the right thing to do.

If you want to learn to do something, you can't be afraid to reach out to experts.

So, if you're just getting started, do like him and network with experts.

Some of his bestselling books are *"The Science of High Performance"* and *"The Mindful Mind"*

Justin Gesso: Justin Gesso is an author, investor, and entrepreneur from Colorado.

He's a 30-something family man with an MBA and a corporate background in product marketing.

His main focus is entrepreneurship and small business ideas.

He consults multi-million dollar companies on their marketing strategies and helps new entrepreneurs get their footing.

I love his story because he went from being a high-paid corporate guy, to entrepreneur, to author.

What I love about his books are the personal stories he shares.

As a family man with a corporate background myself, I love reading about how he broke out of the rat race and found freedom through authorship and entrepreneurship.

His bestselling books are *"Leave the Grind Behind"* and *"Small Business Ideas"*.

Gundi Gabrielle: Gundi Gabrielle is a real inspiration.

She's a highly accomplished conductor, at one point conducting an orchestra for the Pope and at Carnegie Hall.

Performing at that high of a level takes dedication, commitment, passion, and expertise.

And Gundi has it all.

She's left that life behind though and become a self-published author, online entrepreneur, and digital nomad.

Through her books and courses, she shows people how to create thriving online businesses, travel the world, and master social media.

What I think is most unique about her is the attitude and personality she exudes in everything she does, from her book titles, to the covers, down to her company name: Sassy Zen Girl.

I'm not sassy.

I'm not a girl.

And I'm not zen.

But I really like her style and admire her accomplishments.

If you want to succeed, you really should follow her.

Her bestselling books are *"Travel for Free"* and *"The Sassy Way to Social Media Marketing When You Have No Clue"*

Derek Doepker: Derek and I first met in a blog mastermind back in 2010.

It was a mastermind for fitness bloggers and there were about 30 of us that used to share tips with each others.

Derek was a fitness blogger and musician and working on building his online income.

In our mastermind site, he shared how he was making money with Amazon Kindle.

In fact, one of his books make almost $6,000 in 11 days.

It was amazing.

But I didn't have the time to learn yet another thing (I was focused on blogging and SEO) so I didn't pay much attention to it.

Well since then, Derek has written multiple books and is a coach for other authors seeking to sell more books.

He even created a course on Amazon Ads that I bought and partnered with another company to manage Amazon ads for authors.

Derek recently shot a video about how he was able to go from being broke to a successful business owner.

His message was that he started getting results and making money when he focused on *serving* others.

Not solely trying to making money.

And, it's a great point.

His bestselling books are *"Why You're Stuck"* and *"Breakthrough Your BS"*.

Damon Zahariades: Damon is a bestselling author with a corporate background.

I really like him because he writes about productivity and time management.

Something we could ALL use help with.

I love his ambition, hustle, and work ethic.

He shares a great story about waking up and 4 or 5 in the morning to write books when he had his corporate job.

Because he was so passionate about building his business, he kept a very tight schedule.

After he started his business and quit his job, he talks about how his work ethic waned and his passion for waking up early and grinding dipped.

Sadly, his business got smaller and smaller because he spent more time socializing and relaxing than working.

It's sad to hear that story, but it teaches a lesson that hit really close to home for me.

You can't waste your time - and often times when you have very little time, is when you make the most out of it.

Now if he didn't tell that story of how hard he worked when he had no time, and how little he worked when he had lots of time, the message wouldn't have hit home so strongly for me.

THAT'S why I say that stories, personal experiences, and real life examples are so important.

You don't have to be an expert, but you do have to know how to tell great stories.

Because stories stick.

Damon's bestselling books are *"The Art of Saying No"* and *"To-Do List Formula"*

Sally Ann Miller: Sally is a mother, author, and entrepreneur.

I love her style because she's a real person with kids, and family, and a busy life.

She wrote her first book about how she and her family earned passive income by renting their house via Airbnb.

42

I thought that was GREAT concept so I reached out to her.

She also wrote a book about making passive income on Amazon Kindle.

Because that's my niche, I love reading other authors' perspectives because I always learn from them.

Her books are "Make Money on AirBnB", "Make Money as a Life Coach", and "Make Money as a Freelancer".

Kayla Rose Kotecki: Kayla has a really unique story.

She's a former fitness model and bikini competitor.

She used to diet down to like 10% body fat and do photo shoots.

She used to workout all the time and track her diet meticulously.

But in a stunning turn of events, she's left that life and actually is against restrictive diets, neurotic exercise, eating disorders, and body degrading.

It's amazing because she's seen the other side for years and has now decided to speak against it.

She's helping men and women recover from they physical and mental damage and programming that's pushed on them from the media, modern culture, and the health and fitness industry.

She wrote a book called "Damn the Diets" and also has an online course where she helps people get over restrictive eating.

David de las Morenas: David is a former software engineer from Boston, and he's the one that got me into publishing on Kindle.

I found him through his blog and was interested in his topics: fitness and entrepreneurship for men.

I saw that he was a self-published author on Kindle and he actually had a book teaching others how to do the same.

He had written books about fitness, nutrition, motivation, and confidence and was earning a nice passive income from it.

So I bought his book "Write Book, Make Money" and it literally opened up the entire world of Kindle self-publishing to me.

He shared exactly how he wrote and promoted his first book.

It was an absolute game changer for me.

I heard of other people making money on Kindle, but I never thought I could do it.

It seemed too hard, too unattainable.

But after I read his story, and saw the possibilities, I almost became possessed.

It's like something took over me and I saw the potential.

I started taking action and doing exactly what he said in his book.

It wasn't the actual "how to" part that impacted me.

It was his story that impacted me.

I put myself in his shoes, I imagined I was him as I started publishing my first book on Amazon Kindle.

I promoted it as if I were him.

As a result, my first book, "*The Science of Getting Ripped*" became an instant bestseller.

Nick Caldwell: Nick is an energetic father with a young family.

I first found out about him from his book on stress relief.

I liked his style and enthusiasm so I reached out to him.

Since then, we've promoted each other's work, done joint marketing deals, and just given each other feedback and support.

He's a regular guy with a family and a lot of passion.

Some of his books are "*The Selfish Guide to Stress Relief*" and "*The Selfish Workout Guide*".

In the workout book, he talks about how he got in shape despite eating McDonald's everyday.

Although I don't recommend that, what I loved about that is how authentic his story and advice was.

And like I've been saying, that goes a long way.

Anthony Arvanitakis: Now Anthony is another true inspiration.

He's a fitness author with a slew of fantastic books.

He's built an amazing physique with bodyweight workouts.

Oh yeah, he has only one leg.

Now if that isn't a UNIQUE background, I don't know what is.

He's able to take a major life obstacle, and flip it on its head.

He doesn't use his handicap as an excuse, in fact it's his edge.

And he's writing about it and earning a passive income from it.

Some of his best books are *"How to Build Strong and Lean Bodyweight Muscle"* and *"Homemade Muscle"*

Avery Breyer: Avery is a mother of two that quit her job and is now making full-time passive income from her books.

She writes about personal finance, getting out of debt, and earning income via freelance writing.

She has some AMAZINGLY well selling books.

And she got started simply starting.

She didn't have any special advantages or a leg up.

She just researched her market and produced high-quality books.

Now she's able to live in Mexico with her family and enjoy a true passive income lifestyle.

Her bestselling books are *"How to Turn Your Computer Into a Money Machine"* and *"How to Stop Living Paycheck to Paycheck"*

Alykhan Gulamali: I've known Alykhan for a long time.

He's about my age (in his mid 30's) with a family and an IT background from Florida.

He's written about fitness, finance, and happens to be a Microsoft Excel expert.

What I really admire about him is that he's actually given me ideas and taught me a lot over the years.

He taught me how to use the social media site Quora.com to build my audience.

He actually wrote and published an ebook in just 7 days - all by himself. That really inspired me to push myself to create more books.

Some of his books are *"Calorie Counting Secrets"* and *"The Effort Matrix"*

I hope that by reading all of these stories, you feel inspired to take action.

Often times we read articles, or books, or watch videos of people that have had amazing success and think to ourselves:

"I could never do that"

Well, that's a bold faced lie.

Other people just like you have already done it.

So why can't you?

All you have to do is believe that it's possible and take action.

And that's why I wrote this for you.

Chapter 7: The Two Most Common Approaches

Let me ask you a question.

What do the following movies have in common?

The Karate Kid

The Matrix

Terminator 2

The Last Samurai

The Lego Movie

Boiler Room

The Wizard of Oz

Big Hero 6

Home Alone

Aladdin

Fight Club

Star Wars

Forrest Gump

American History X

Gladiator

Batman

The Jungle Book

Scarface

Braveheart

Kill Bill

The Lord of the Rings

The Notebook

If you guessed that they are all macho movies (with the exception of The Notebook), you'd be right.

But that isn't the answer I'm looking for.

The answer is the the main character(s) in each of these movies had some sort of transformation.

They started with some kind of dilemma, some kind of challenge, some twist of fate that took them from their comfortable life down the road of an epic saga.

Often times it was hoisted upon them, by no fault of their own.

And that's why we fall in love with these movies.

It's a classic writing formula called "the hero's journey" and it's what makes us fall in love with movies and characters.

Maybe because we see a bit of ourselves in the characters.

We identify with their fears, their struggles, and their eventual triumph.

Why am I talking about this?

Because like I said earlier, people want to hear your story.

They don't just want "how to" content.

They want to hear your story, how you overcame their challenges, how you overcame roadblocks, how you overcame obstacles.

Because they are afraid of hitting those same roadblocks.

So if you can write a really, really good book documenting your story, it WILL resonate with people.

Kind of like I'm doing in this book.

Some people just "pump and dump" books on Amazon Kindle.

They write 40, 50, 60, even 100 books on Amazon.

Actually, they pay someone to write those books on Amazon for them.

They do make money.

Some books make $10 per month.

Some books make $100 per month.

Altogether, these people make $5k to $10k per month.

It's great money and they're earning it passively.

But it's a LOT of work to go through all of that.

Often times, they're obscure topics like essential oils, how to have a deeper voice, how to have firmer thighs, etc.

Now they make money, but the author is usually using a pen name and isn't developing him or herself as an authority.

I mean, how can you be an expert in anything when you write about 50 different topics?

Sure, that's one way to go about it, but I don't recommend it.

That's kind of the way that people used to do article marketing on the internet years and years ago.

They would write a bunch of low-quality articles focused specifically on very highly searched keywords that they would hope would rank highly in the Google.

If you know anything about content farms and what's happened to article directories, you'll know that the traffic that a lot of these little articles used to bring has really been wiped out by Google.

Google had a bunch of updates a few years ago that really just crushed all of these sites that allowed users to write these skimpy little articles on specific keywords.

What Google has ended up favoring is long, authoritative, highly detailed, well researched, and very interlinked articles that link out to other authoritative resources.

We're going to use that exact same strategy to publish your Kindle books.

You want to write authoritative books that are 50 to 100 pages long.

In terms of word count, if you write a Word document, like a Microsoft Word document, and if it's anywhere between 12.000 and 20,000 words, you're golden.

That's going to help you get more money from Kindle's program where they pay you per the amount of pages that your readers read, and it'll help you as far as browsers who are just browsing and looking at your book.

If they see a book that's between 50 and 100 pages they're going to feel more compelled to buy it, as compared to a book that's maybe 200 or 300 pages because they want a quick solution usually.

That's the way that you want to write books, and that's the strategy that I recommend when writing books.

Yeah, you can write 50 or 100 books. You can either write them yourself, or you can hire a ghostwriter to write them for you, and it'll take you about a year or so to get that many books published on Kindle.

Yes, if you research your keywords correctly, you will make somewhere between $5,000 and $10,000, but if you use a strategy of writing more authoritative, well-researched and very well-marketed books, you can make way more money than that.

For example, in my book, "*The Science of Getting Ripped*", I wrote a book that ended up being 182 pages on Kindle. In Microsoft Word, it was only about 80 pages, but the way it was formatted and spaced translated into about 182 pages on Kindle.

When I wrote that book, I marketed it to my email list. I had an email list of about 2,500 subscribers, so that gave me a little bit of a boost.

Then I marketed it on a bunch of other sites that promote discounted Kindle books. When I did that, Amazon saw that a lot of people are buying this book, and it became an instant bestseller in the men's health category and the weight training category.

Once it became a bestseller, people naturally found my book because people tend to find and look at the bestseller charts to see what the hottest new books are so that they can buy them. Also, Amazon starts promoting your book themselves as a hot new release.

I was able to make a decent amount of money from selling my book just by writing a really authoritative, long book, and marketing it really well.

On top of that, if you have an authoritative book like that, readers are more likely to leave you reviews. I've gotten multiple, unsolicited, completely natural and organic reviews, because the book was actually something that people read and took seriously, and felt compelled to leave a positive review for.

On top of that, when you have an authoritative book, you've already proven yourself, and proven the type of quality that you can create. Then it makes it much easier for people to join your email list. In the front of my book and in the back of my book, I ask people to join my email newsletter.

Because I've written such a good book, and such an impactful and authoritative book, people trust me more, and because they trust me, they're willing to join my email list.

If you don't know already, once someone joins your email list, especially after they've made a purchase from you, they're more likely to make future purchases from you.

I remember my marketing professor in college telling us that it is 3 to 5 to 7 times more expensive to get a new customer, compared to taking someone who's already a customer and convincing them to buy more products from you.

That's why you want to write a really good, impactful, authoritative book, sell it for, let's say, $2.99 on Kindle, and once they buy your book, you want to entice them to join your email list.

Once they join your email list, they're already fans of your work and of your writing, and they already trust you, and they'll be more likely and more willing to buy your future books, and that's where the real money is made.

On top of that, you can promote other people's books as an affiliate. In my example with my fitness book, The Science of Getting Ripped, not only can I promote other books that I've written, I can also promote books that are in a similar industry as mine, other fitness books or diet-related books.

If you go to websites like ClickBank.com, you'll find tons and tons of e-books that sell for anywhere from $40 to $100, because these are comprehensive programs, digital programs or eBook programs.

Their sales pages are written by some of the best copywriters in the world, so all you have to do is send an email to your email subscribers, recommending one of these products, and then let the vendor do the selling on your behalf.

Not only that, you can sell other Amazon products to your email subscribers. Like I said, I've written a fitness book, *"The Science of Getting Ripped"*, and I can email my email subscribers recommendations of other fitness products that they can buy right on Amazon.

Amazon is one of the most trusted websites in the entire world, and people have no problem just clicking the buy with 1 click button, because they have their credit cards already stored on file with Amazon.com.

I can send an email to my email list of supplements that I recommend that are sold on Amazon.

I can send them links to products on Amazon like weight-lifting clothes, home gyms, other books, other fitness equipment, and the list goes on and on.

As you can see, just from one book, one little book that I really poured my heart and soul into, that I really wrote with the intention of really helping my readers solve a specific problem, I'm able to make multiple income streams it, whether it's my own products or other people's products, or even physical products that are sold on Amazon.com.

The beauty of selling other people's products is that I can make an affiliate commission if my email subscribers buy these products.

Not only that, I can continue to make money by offering higher-ticket items, like maybe one-on-one coaching. For my fitness book, I can ask my email subscribers if they'd like to pay me for one-on- one monthly coaching.

Actually, my wife is a dietitian, and I've offered my wife's dietitian services to my email subscribers as another way to make passive income.

On top of that, you can even hold live events or online webinars, where you charge your email subscribers or you charge your customers to pay you for an online event or even a live, in-person event.

As you can see, as opposed to writing 100 books on weird, obscure, not very savory topics, you can write a book on, let's say, fitness, or you can write a book on time management, or you can write a book on parenting tips, or you can write a book on nutrition, or you can write a book on eco-friendly living, and really pour your heart and soul into it, and build a strong, six-figure business after you ask your readers to join your email list.

That's the way that I recommend to make money on Kindle.

Chapter 8: The Simple, Repeatable Process I Used to LAUNCH My Passive Income Machine - In 10 Hours

Ok, now let's get to the meat and potatoes of this book.

The actual mechanics of HOW to write and sell a book on Kindle that generates passive income.

But rather than give you a dry, generic, outdated formula, I'm going to share what I did.

I'll share each of the steps I took to write my book.

That's what makes this book different from the other ones on the market.

It also makes it easier for me to write :)

Because if I show you my steps, you can simulate my results.

I'll share my tips, my resources, my secrets, and my tricks.

If you use them, you **will** be successful.

To get started, you want to go to kdp.amazon.com and register.

That is the Kindle Direct Publishing site and it's where you're going to upload your book.

I won't go in detail on that site, because if you're computer literate and follow the instructions, you'll easily be able to upload your book and publish it in 10 minutes.

If you struggle, you can always check their "Help" section.

I want to spend my time showing you how to make the book an instant bestseller that generates passive income right out of the gate.

And that's what I'm going to do.

Chapter 9: How to Write Your Bestselling Book - In Just 7 Days

I'm going to challenge you to write your book in 7 days.

I know it sounds crazy.

But it's completely doable.

It comes down to having a really solid outline.

Because once you know what you want to write, putting it all on paper is really, really easy.

Even if you can't type!

At first thought, writing a book sounds like a daunting task.

I know because I felt that myself.

But I'm going to share a secret that works really, really well for me.

Creating an outline.

If you have an idea in your mind for a book that you want to write or if you have a topic that you'd like to write about, the biggest piece of advice that I can give you is to just put your pen to paper and write the book.

So don't make it harder than it is and just do it.

In fact, I'm writing this book in February of 2018, but I actually had the idea and outline back in June of 2016.

I waited a year and a half to actually write this book because I allowed myself to make a mountain out of a molehill.

But now I'm almost done and it took less than two weeks (if that)

In the coming pages, I'm going to show you a really easy way to do that, but I can't stress how important it is for you to begin writing and to finish your book, because believe it or not, it's not that hard.

But first, think of what you want to write about.

It should be something that people care about.

A certain professional skill like programming or project management.

A certain life skill like public speaking or resolving conflict.

A certain physical skill like knitting or writing fiction books.

Or a personal transformation like how you've traveled the world without spending tons of money or how you battled and overcame addiction or got in shape.

The point is that you have to write about something that people care about.

And Amazon is amazing for telling you what people care about.

The way to do that is to browse the bestseller categories (and subcategories) and see what's selling.

Look at the covers.

Look at the titles.

Look at the descriptions.

Look at the reviews.

The last thing you want to do is write something that nobody wants.

Luckily, with Amazon you can see what's selling in real-time and make sure that your book incorporates some of those elements.

If you're struggling, then make a list of at least 10 things that you can teach others.

Narrow it down to the top 3 that you think would help people the most.

Then, think about the 1 BEST topic that you can write about.

It should be something that you have personal experience with.

People LOVE stories, so be sure that you can include your own challenges, struggles, and eventual triumphs.

Because **THAT'S** what people want to read.

The Easiest Way to Write Your Book

For your outline, you want to list out 7 to 15 chapter headings.

Under each chapter, you want to create three sub-chapters, and under each of those three sub-chapters, you want to create three main points.

Here's how it would look:

> ### Chapter 1
>
> **Subchapter 1**
>
> -main point 1
>
> -main point 2
>
> -main point 3
>
> **Subchapter 2**
>
> -main point 1
>
> -main point 2
>
> -main point 3
>
> **Subchapter 3**
>
> -main point 1
>
> -main point 2
>
> -main point 3
>
> **Chapter 2** (do the same as above)

Can you see how you're starting to put together the structure of your book very easily, systematically, and methodically?

In fact, there's a great free software online called MindMup.com

It really helps you visualize the entire book.

Here's how my mind map looks on MindMup.com for this book:

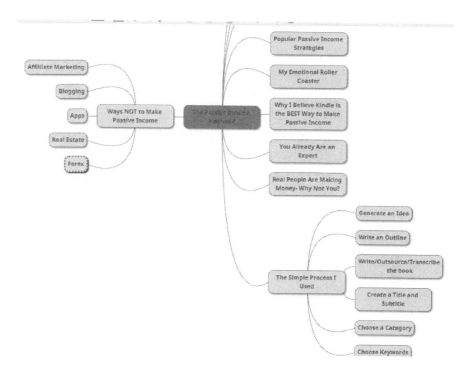

You can drill down even further than I did.

The beauty of this process is that it allows you to see everything at once, which will generate more and more ideas.

The key is to dump every story, fact, lesson, personal experience, struggle, and idea that you can into the outline.

Because the more you put, the easier and easier the book is going to be to write.

That's what I did when I started my book *"The Science of Getting Ripped"*

I documented how I got in shape.

I even searched articles from big websites and copied and pasted the main points into my outline.

Not because I was plagiarizing them.

But because I liked the way they worded it.

So I would make sure I changed it and rewrote it to fit my experiences.

Also, it would help get my juices flowing so I could start expanding on the point myself.

In no time, I had an outline that was ready to be written.

That's how creating an outline makes writing a book so easy.

Starting with 7 to 10 chapters, that gets you thinking about what you want to write about and then writing your three sub-chapters and then three main topics under each sub-chapter helps you think even more.

Then under each sub-chapter, adding three main points helps you drill down really gradually.

This shouldn't take more than one or two hours, and once you have that, you have the skeleton of your next bestselling book.

Action Item: Start the outline of your book. List out 7-10 chapters. Then list out 3 sub-chapters in each chapter. Then list 3 main points that you want to talk about under each sub-chapter. You can add more notes and info under each section.

Now you have the makings of your book. On to the next step...

3 Tricks to TURBOCHARGE Your Results

Now that you have your chapters, your sub-chapters, and your three main points under each sub-chapter written, the next thing for you to do is to start writing the body content.

Trick #1: Dictating Your Book:

What I did with my very first book, *The Science of Getting Ripped*, was that I started dictating my book.

I'm a busy guy with three kids and a full-time job, and a two-hour daily commute, and a demanding IT job in a hospital.

I don't have a lot of time to sit down and write, but after I had my outline and my sub-chapters and my main points under my sub-chapters, all I had to do was pick up my iPhone, turn on the voice recording app, and start speaking out what I wanted to write.

Instantly, I was able to use my two-hour daily commute and idle time when I was sitting in the car or sitting at home, I was able to make that productive by looking at my outline and dictating my book into the audio file in my iPhone.

Once I had that, I was able to submit it to a voice-to-text transcribing company, and I recommend:

•**Rev.com**: They're my **FAVORITE** and only charge $1 per minute, best of all, they turn the transcription around to you in less than 24 hours.

•**Dragon Anywhere**: This iPhone app costs $15/month.

Transcribing your books is amazing and a complete game changer.

But I still like writing.

As long as I have a solid outline, I can easily start writing the book.

Trick #2: Write in Short Sentences

Another absolute game changer is how you write.

If you notice, I write in short paragraphs.

Each paragraph is only one or two sentences.

This is on purpose.

When I write like that, I feel more conversational.

I'm able to see the words that I've just written, and I can then build upon them very quickly.

Almost like I'm having a conversation with a friend.

Using this method, I can easily write 1000 words in less than an hour.

Sometimes I can write close to 2000 words.

At this pace, I can get a 10,000 word book written in 5 days.

Trick #3: Hire a Ghostwriter:

Another option is to get it written by a ghostwriter.

But, I DON'T recommend that you have a ghostwriter create low quality book that you just publish.

If you use a ghostwriter, be sure to put your own spin on the book.

Have a unique angle.

Add your own story.

Once we have your book transcribed and sent back to you, you need to edit the book.

No matter how you write the book, you need to edit it for content and grammar.

I've skipped this step in previous books and it's resulted in negative reviews on Amazon.

I know it sucks to have to hire an editor, but just do it.

You can find people that will edit for $1 per page.

If you don't want to do that, you can ask your friends and family to read the book and give you their feedback, or you can go on websites like Fiverr or Odesk and pay someone to edit the book for you, both for grammar and for content.

But please, hire an editor so the book is polished.

Action Item:

Sit down and start writing your outline.

Just get it done because once you do, writing the entire book will seem way less daunting.

After that, you should write for one hour a day.

If you can write 1000 words per hour, you'll have the book done in 10 days.

Even that's too long.

Open your phone and start dictating your book. You can choose to type it out as well, but if you have very little time, dictating will help tremendously.

I prefer Rev.com, because they're very fast and accurate, but it's totally up to you.

Just think about that for a second. Let's say that you dictate into your phone for 60 minutes. You simply pay $60 and you have the makings of your next bestselling book.

It's absolutely amazing, and at that pace, you can write a book a week, but it all comes back down to having a solid outline, sub-chapters, and main points under your sub-chapters.

Chapter 10: The Secret to Grabbing Their Attention with an AMAZING Title and Subtitle

You can have the best book in the world, but if no one buys it, you'll never make money from it.

That's why your hook is so important.

What's a hook?

It's what makes the book unique.

It's what grabs people's attention so they want to look at it and buy it.

It's your unique message to the world

It's what makes you different.

Your hook has to address an emotional need.

It has to speak to a problem that the person is having.

It has to convey something so cool, unique, and earth-shattering, that they have no choice but to buy your book.

Think about the iPod.

When it first came out, there were other MP3 players.

But none of them sold as well as the iPod.

Why?

Because of the hook.

Apple marketed the iPod by saing *"1,000 songs in your pocket"*

Powerful.

When I was writing *"The Science of Getting Ripped"*, I was wondering what I should call it.

At first I was going to call it *"Inner Strength, Functional Physique"*.

Because I wanted to convey how working out isn't just about looking good and being strong, it's about inner strength.

But if I called it that, it wouldn't have sold.

Then I thought of **The Lean Muscle Secret/Formula/Solution: How to Get Ripped in 90 Days**

Better, but it still didn't have a ring to it.

I finally settled on "**The Science of Getting Ripped**: *Proven Workout Tricks and Diet Hacks to Build Muscle and Burn Fat in Half the Time*"

Here's why it worked: it had a catchy title. It used copywriting power words "hack" and "tricks". It made a promise. And it made it time specific.

So you HAVE to think of a hook.

The hook is even more important than the actual content if you want to sell.

Because you're going to use your hook in the title and subtitle.

And top copywriters will tell you that they spend 80% of their time writing a good headline.

That's how important your hook/headline/title are.

Because if a browser looks at your title and isn't interested, he or she will just move on and never buy your book.

Of course, the content HAS to be good, but if you ignore the hook, no one will buy it.

Make it emotional.

Make it gripping.

Make it powerful.

Struggling to find good ideas?

Look at the classics and timeless best sellers:

Switch

No Easy Day

Thug Kitchen

Skinny Bitch

Skinny Bitch in the Kitch

How to Win Friends and Influence People

Deep Work

The One Thing

The Blue Ocean Strategy

Rich Dad, Poor Dad

The Art of the Deal

The Millionaire Next Door

The Four Hour Work Week

The Subtle Art of Not Giving a F*ck

The Life-Changing Magic of Tidying Up

The 7 Habits of Highly Effective People

How to Think Like a Spy

Blink

Freakonomics

Think about these titles.

What imagery do they conjure up?

What emotions do they engage?

What do you perceive about the book?

So you HAVE to have a strong title and hook.

If you don't, the book won't do well.

It should imply "how to" or a transformation because THAT'S what people are buying.

One last story that I want to leave you with is about the classic bestseller, "*Think and Grow Rich*"

When Napoleon Hill first wrote it in the 1930's he called it "*The Philosophy of Success*" but it didn't sell very well.

Then he renamed it "*The Science of Personal Achievement*" and it still didn't sell well.

Then he named it "*Think and Grow Rich*" and it has sold over 100 million copies.

In fact, I have a book called "*17 Quick and Easy High-Protein Meals*" and it hasn't sold well.

So I just retitled it to "*Eat This, Burn Fat: 17 Wickedly Simple Meals to Build Muscle, Burn Fat, and Get Ripped*"

I suspect it will sell much better.

For subtitles, I recommend the following:

- Call out a specific audience demographic
- Describe the benefits the reader will get by reading the book
- Address a specific pain the reader is experiencing
- Make a specific promise to the reader

For example, here are sub-titles from my books:

- *Proven Diet Hacks and Workout Tricks to Burn Fat and Build Muscle in Half the Time*
- *15 Scientifically Proven Habits to Build Mental Toughness and a High Performance Mindset*
- *The Scientifically Proven Method to Relieve Stress, Melt Tension, and Gain Peace of Mind in 5 Minutes a Day*
- *The Step-by-Step Guide to Supercharge Your Productivity and Crush Your Goals in the Next 30 Days*

You get the idea.

Make it gripping so your readers that NOTICE.

Action Item:

Top copywriters often write 25 different headlines when they begin writing an ad or salesletter.

And I want you to do the same.

In fact, I did the same when I came up with the title for this book.

I didn't want to, but my mentors said I really should.

So I did and I'm so glad that I did.

It's not hard to do.

Just sit down and crank out 25 different titles.

As you write them, you'll get more and more ideas.

Then the next day, you should see if you have any more ideas.

Then finally, you should choose the one you like best.

Chapter 11: A Picture is Worth a 1000 Words - How to Create Your Bestselling Cover

After your title and subtitle, your cover is the most important factor in selling your book.

Just like the title and subtitle, it helps to really look at other best sellers.

As you do, you'll start to notice a trend.

Big words.

Compelling images.

Lots of empty space.

Contrasting colors.

I really like the cover of the book *"The Tipping Point"* by Malcolm Gladwell.

The image of the match hints at a spark creating a fire.

Just look at what covers you like and get one designed that has those elements that you like.

As for creating the covers, here are a few places I recommend:

- **Fiverr.com**: You'll get amazing looking covers from Fiverr. It's surprising how many good cover designers there are on this site.

- **99Designs.com**: I've never used this site, but I know a lot of other publishers do. You'll get great designers here.

- **Canva.com**: If you want to create your own cover, I recommend using Canva. I've done it myself and I really like what I came up with

For *"The Science of Getting Ripped"* I spent about $50 on my cover.

Just like with titles and subtitles, I also recommend creating a few different covers.

Make them completely different colors, themes, designs, imagery, etc.

Then test them using a site called PickFu.com

On PickFu, they have people that will look at your covers and give you their feedback.

So if you submit two covers, you can pay to have 50 people vote on which one they like best.

They'll often give you feedback on what they like, what they don't like, and their suggestions.

They're really cheap; like $20 for 50 voters to rate your design.

Action Item:

Use one of the sites above to create at least two different covers.

Then submit them to PickFu (or your friends and family on social media) to see which one they like best.

Chapter 12: "Sell the Sizzle, Not the Steak" - How to Write an AWESOME Description

Writing a good description is really important too.

You don't have to master the art of copywriting, but you DO have to focus on 3 things: emotion, imagery, story.

By now your title, subtitle, and cover will have grabbed the reader's attention.

The description is where you elaborate on it.

Rattle their emotions about their current state and paint a beautiful picture of how things will look in the future

Promise a solution with imagery of what life will look like.

Be sure to use these words (they're some of the most powerful words in the English language)

- You
- Free
- Instantly
- Because
- Secret
- Reveal
- Discover
- Mind-blowing
- Quick
- Easy
- Revolutionary
- Proven
- Guaranteed
- Immediately
- Breakthrough
- Unique
- Surprising
- Hidden
- Forbidden

Your description should identify what the user is thinking, the pain they're feeling, the problem they want solved.

Then it should promise them a solution that make them want to buy your book.

Want to know a secret to understand what your reader is thinking and what they want?

Read reviews of other books in your niche.

This is absolute gold.

Reading reviews will give you insight into what your readers like and dislike about those books.

You'll be able to empathize with them and truly understand what it is that they're looking for.

That's what I've done for my previous books, and what I'm doing for this book.

Once you know what your audience wants, then use those same exact words in your description.

It will resonate with them so strongly!

I love using bullet points and **bold** and <u>underlined</u> text in my descriptions because they improve readability.

Lastly, include a call to action at the end saying something like "Get your copy now"

If you're struggling, then simply look at some other bestselling books in your niche.

Action Item:

Read descriptions of 5 other books in your niche.

Look at the wording, sentence structure, and style and then write your own draft.

Be sure to use bold and underlined text.

Lastly, read reviews of other books in your genre and incorporate those points in your description.

Chapter 13: How to Choose Keywords for Your Book

Amazon allows you to choose up to 7 keywords for your book.

I usually choose the most logical keywords for my niche.

For "*The Science of Getting Ripped*" I chose pretty logical ones:

- How to get ripped
- How to burn fat and build muscle
- Burn fat
- Workouts for men
- etc.

And I would rank in the Amazon Kindle search engine for those keywords.

You want to put them in the keyword section of the Kindle Direct Publishing platform and use them naturally in your description.

I still do that for every book I write.

And one amazing way to find keywords is to simply type keywords into the Amazon Kindle search bar.

Do it slowly and you'll notice that Amazon suggests keywords.

Use them - because if Amazon is suggesting them to you, they're suggesting them to their millions and millions of customers.

But over time, I stopped paying so much attention to them.

Sure they're important, but I don't personally believe they're the end-all-be-all.

I know other authors feel differently.

And they probably have very good reasons.

I just haven't seen it being terribly useful.

In other words, if I'm writing quick little books that I want to rank for specific keywords, then they ARE valuable.

If I'm writing an authority book with an emotional hook, in a hot niche, addressing a very relevant problem, then I don't worry about keywords as much.

Some of the most successful authors I see on Amazon Kindle write really, really good books that don't rely on keywords.

For example, Peter Voogd wrote a book called "*6 Months to 6 Figures*" which is a GREAT title.

Within a month he was making over $20,000.

And it wasn't from keywords.

Action Item:

Keywords are important, and you should utilize the 7 that Amazon allows you to enter, but I personally don't spend too much time on this.

Be sure to use your keywords in your description.

Chapter 14: Choosing the Right Category - The SECRET to Getting TONS of Exposure

Choosing the right category is CRITICAL because if you put your book in too competitive of a

category, it will never see the light of day.

This is one of the MOST important parts of setting up your Kindle book.

Now Amazon Kindle has TONS of categories and sub-categories.

The way to make your book an instant bestseller is to choose a very niche sub-category.

My thinking when I launched my book is that if I can get onto the first page of my category, people will start to find me naturally - and they did.

Besides, a sales rank category of 10k means that you're selling 5-10 copies of your book per day - which is TOTALLY doable

And if your book is priced at $2.99, that's $10 to $20 per day, or $300 to $600 per month - passively.

Often times you can make much more.

So once I was on the first page, I kept promoting my book so it climbed higher and higher, until it eventually became a bestseller

Don't worry, I'll share more on how I did that later in the "Launch" section of this book

But understanding how categories is SO important because once you become a best seller, Amazon starts to promote you.

They promote you in the Mover and Shakers section and in the Hot New Releases section.

And when they do that, you start getting more and more sales.

So let's discuss categories on Amazon Kindle.

Here's the listing of main categories in the Kindle store:

‹ Any Department

‹ Kindle Store

Kindle eBooks

Arts & Photography

Biographies & Memoirs

Business & Money

Children's eBooks

Comics & Graphic Novels

Computers & Technology

Cookbooks, Food & Wine

Crafts, Hobbies & Home

Education & Teaching

Engineering &
Transportation

Foreign Languages

Health, Fitness & Dieting

History

Humor & Entertainment

Law

Lesbian, Gay, Bisexual &
Transgender eBooks

Literature & Fiction

Medical eBooks

Mystery, Thriller &
Suspense

Nonfiction

Parenting & Relationships

Politics & Social Sciences

Reference

Religion & Spirituality

Romance

Science & Math

Science Fiction & Fantasy

Self-Help

Sports & Outdoors

Teen & Young Adult

Travel

If you drill down, you'll see even more sub-categories.

This is where the gold is.

Because if you can write a book and sell enough copies, you'll become a bestseller.

Here's an example of the "Men's Health" category that I ranked #1 in for months.

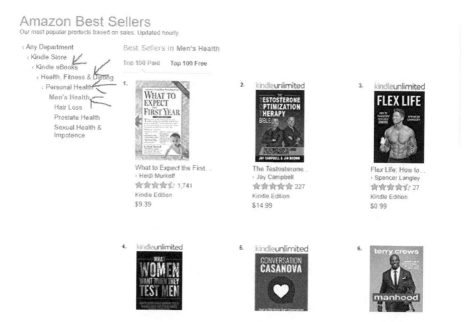

You can see that *"What to Expect the First Year"* is #1 in the Kindle eBooks → Health, Fitness, and Dieting → Personal Health → Men's Health subcategory.

The trick is to find a very niche category that you can dominate so that you become a bestseller.

When that happens, people will be more inclined to buy, which will increase your sales rank, allowing you to switch your book into more competitive categories.

Now from my personal experience, if you can sell just 15 copies of a book per day, you can become a bestseller in certain subcategories.

And once you do, Amazon gives you a "bestseller" symbol which gives you more authority and visibility within your category.

So your goal is to make as many sales as possible so that you quickly become a bestseller in your subcategory, and then people that are browsing those categories naturally find you.

That's when you want to raise the price as well.

Now Amazon allows you to choose only 2 categories, so it's a good idea to be in two different categories so you get more exposure.

For example, if you write a cookbook, put your book in the Cooking category and the Health, Fitness, and Dieting category (and respective subcategories) so you get views from readers browsing both sections

Or if you're writing a time management book, put it in the Self-Help category and the Business and Money category (and respective subcategories) so you get exposure from readers that are interested in both Self-Help books and Business books about productivity.

So you want to look for niche categories that you can DOMINATE.

Here's an example of a niche category:

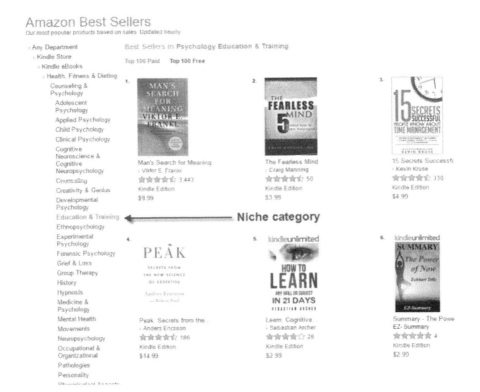

Action Item: Dig deep into the categories and subcategories on Amazon and list out 3 categories that you could put your book into.

The #3 book in your category should be sales rank of 20,000 or higher. If it's any lower than that, the category is too competitive.

Here is the specific ranking of this book:

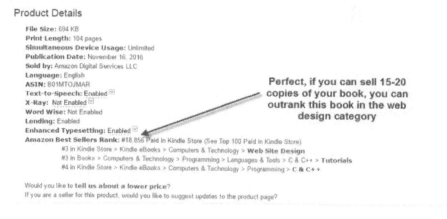

Hunting for categories is crucial – as you sell more copies, you can move into more competitive categories.

The best thing is that you can switch categories as often as you want.

I've seen people change their books to differently subcategories on a monthly, and even weekly basis.

There's no reason you can't do the same.

Chapter 15: How to Price Your Book So It Makes TONS of Sales

This is going to be a short chapter.

I advise pricing your book at 99 cents to begin with.

Why?

Because you want to get lots of exposure very fast.

Like the US Special Forces says, you want to rely on surprise, speed, and violence of action.

(I obviously don't mean physical violence)

What I mean is that you want to price your book so low, and market it so aggressively, that casual browsers are intrigued enough to buy it on the spot.

This is so important because they more sales you get within a specific time period, the higher your book will be ranked in your category.

And Amazon recalculates the bestseller rankings every few hours.

For example, if you get 50-100 sales in one day, you could easily hit an Amazon Best Seller Rank of 5,000 or below.

The more books you sell, the lower your rank.

So the top selling book on all of the Kindle store is ranked #1.

The second bestselling book on the Kindle store is ranked #2.

And so on.

So if you're ranked 4000 on all of the Kindle store, that means you're the 5000th bestselling book on Amazon.

And that's a HUGE achievement.

That's why I recommend pricing the book at 99 cents when you first publish it.

You want to get as much exposure and reviews as possible.

After that you can gradually increase the price by $1 per week.

When I first launched "*The Science of Getting Ripped*", I started at 99 cents, and then once I was done with my promotions and it was a bestseller, I increased the price to $1.99, then $2.99, then $3.99, and finally $4.99.

The beauty of doing is is that while your book is a bestseller at 99 cents, people still have the option of buying your paperback book.

So your Kindle version will only be 99 cents, but the paperback version will be much, much more.

When I published my paperback version, I priced it at $14.99 and then increased it to $19.9

Now, some people recommend launching your book for free.

Amazon Kindle gives you the option to drop your price to free for 5 days within a 90 day period, if you sign up for their KDP Select program.

The idea is that you promote your book for free, get tons of downloads (I've gotten thousands of downloads on my books before), and then when it comes back to regular price, you'll get more sales because of the exposure.

That has never worked for me.

If I had a book that wasn't selling, doing a free promo got me lots of downloads, but the book wasn't ranked any higher when it returned back to normal price.

Action Item:

Just launch your book for 99 cents.

Be sure to have a paperback version available as well so that you make higher royalties.

Then bump your price up to $2.99 once you've finished your launch.

Chapter 16: GO! GO! GO! How to Launch Your Book and Make LOTS of Money

-Use my email to Nadhir

-Use Sally Ann Miller's super simple launch strategy

-Use the 5 day launch plan from Steve Scott

Believe it or not, that was the easy part, because now we're going to focus on promoting your book.

By far, marketing and promoting and selling your book is 80% of the work.

I spent so much time researching, investigating and comparing different marketing and advertising strategies, and I wanted to share those with you today in this post.

There are two ways to promote a book; promote it as a free book or promote it as a paid book.

Free Promo Case Study

First, let me go over a very common and popular promotional strategy, which is to release a book for free.

Now, a lot of people say that this is what you should do, and I actually did the same thing.

I've taken a lot of courses and read a lot of articles and even bought books on how to publish and promote an Amazon Kindle, and most of them had said to release your book for free.

The thinking behind it is that you write a book, you promote it for free, you get a lot of exposure, and then you switch the price and make it into a paid book.

This used to work maybe three years ago, but there are a couple of problems with it today.

Look at the screen shots that I have below. I've gotten over 7,000 downloads in a single day for my books, but very few subsequent sales after I decided to switch them to being a paid book.

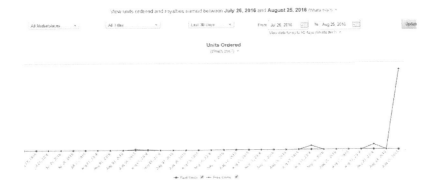

And I got ranked VERY highly in the free store:

Now, out of 7,000 free downloads, if I would have gotten 500 or even 400, even 200 or even 100 email subscribers, I would have thought it's worthwhile.

But I got less than 20 email subscribers, so it was not worth it to me at all. I'm not saying that it doesn't work for anyone, but I've tried it and in my testing and in my experience, it doesn't work nearly as well as people may have you think.

That's why I recommend doing a paid launch, meaning, launch the book for 99 cents.

Which brings me to my next case study…

Paid Promo Case Study

Here's what I found to really work, and it comes down to releasing your book as a paid book.

Even if you release a book for 99 cents, I've found that the perceived value is much higher than if you were to release a book and promote it for free.

I was able to become a bestseller in the Men's Health category.

And in the weight training category.

Now, I never got thousands of even hundreds of downloads or sales, but I was able to make anywhere between 10 and 20 sales a day for months following this strategy.

What is this strategy that I used to release my book or to promote my book?

Well the first thing I did is I made sure that the book was 99 cents. Then, here's what I did:

- I sent an email to my email list offering the book to them, telling them that it's a limited time discount where I'm offering the book for 99 cents.

- Then, I promoted it on Bknights on Fiverr for $5

- Then I promoted it on Buck Books, and I was shocked, it was huge. I made 90 sales and that was a major tipping point for me. They only charge $29 for a promo.

- Then I promoted it on Bookzio and got a few sales

- Then on ReadingDeals

- Then on BooksButterfly

- And then on BargainBooksy

This is the EXACT strategy I used to become a bestseller in multiple categories.

Here are the results I was able to achieve:

- I became a bestseller in the men's health and the training niches or categories on Amazon Kindle.

- I got almost 40 positive reviews

- I got a steady stream of 3-5 email subscribers per day

- I made steady sales for months and months which motivated me to write and publish other books

Maybe it's because people take the book more seriously because they're actually spending real money on it, but using this strategy has been WAY more successful than promoting the book for free.

Action Item: Stagger your promotions using the sites I listed above. If you have an email list, email them first, then ask your friends and family to purchase. Then use the promo sites I mentioned above.

You want to show Amazon that your book is selling well over multiple days so that you can get listed in their "Hot New Releases" and "Mover and Shaker" section. Essentially, if you promote your book well, then Amazon will start promoting YOU. And believe me, that is AWESOME.

Also, once you're a best seller, you stay up high in the rankings and people start to find you organically.

Now, I didn't make much money, but the idea was to get a lot of exposure and then raise the price in hopes of people finding my book naturally as they browsed the categories on Amazon.

Here's a very simple launch plan you can follow to give your book a HUGE boost in sales so that it becomes a bestseller and starts selling naturally.

Price it at 99 cents. I've found that promoting a book for free doesn't yield much in terms of paid sales.

Here are the sites that I recommend. I have used almost all of them and

- Your own email list and social media following
- BKnight on Fiverr; I usually get 15 sales
- **BuckBooks.com**; I usually get 60 sales
- **eReaderIQ.com**; I get 70-90 sales
- **BargainBooksy.com**; I get 25-50 sales
- **BargainEbookHunter.com**
- **EReaderNewsToday.com**
- **ManyBooks.com**
- **Robin Reads**
- **OHFB.com**
- **BookRunes.com**
- **EBookHound.com**
- **Bookzio.com**
- **BookRaid.com**; I get 10-20 sales
- **TheFussyLibrarian.com**; I get 10-20 sales
- **ChoosyBookworm.com**; I get about 25-30 sales

Schedule 2-3 promotions on consecutive days so that you have a nice amount of sales each day.

Doing that will show Amazon that your book is selling and they might promote it as a "Hot New Release".

I would also space them out a bit for maximum effect.

For example, promote it for a few days at 99 cents then bump the price up to $2.99. Then if sales drop a bit, lower the price to 99 cents again and promote on a few more sites until your sales rank lowers and you make more natural sales. Then you can bump the price up to $2.99 again.

Here's the thing, in most categories, if you just get 80 sales in 1 day, you'll be in the top 5. So if you can schedule two of these promos per day, on consecutive days, plus email your list, you'll build enough momentum to be an instant best-seller. After that, you'll be at the top of the charts, and people will naturally find you and buy your book. **The trick is to make sure your cover and title are captivating.**

Again, schedule a promo on BKnight one day, then BargainBooksy the second day, and then ManyBooks the third day, then increase the price to $2.99. Then a few days later lower it to 99 cents and do a promo with BookRaid, then Bookzio, then OHFB.

To get ongoing sales, you can use pay-per-click ads like Amazon Marketing Services or BookBub ads but that's outside the scope of this book.

If you want to learn about that, just look up Dave Chesson's free Kindlepreneur Amazon Marketing Services course.

Chapter 17: How to Get Your First 10 Reviews

Reviews are an essential part of selling your book long term.

And honestly, it's what I struggle with the most.

In general, 1 in 50 readers will leave a review for you.

So you have to ask for them often.

In the beginning and the end of your book.

Even then, you won't get many.

So in the beginning, you have to make a list of all of your friends and family that will support you and your book.

Email them asking them if they can buy the book and leave a review when it's priced at 99 cents.

It's important that they actually buy the book because their review will be "verified review" which counts more in Amazon's algorithm.

So in the beginning you need to get as many as you can.

Be sure to read Amazon's review guidelines so that you don't break any of their rules.

Because they have been known to delete reviews that they suspect of being fake or bought.

I know people that had dozens and dozens of reviews deleted.

So be careful and know the rules.

When I first released "*The Science of Getting Ripped*" my goal was to get 7 reviews.

I reached out to friends, family, and my email list.

Another amazing way to get reviews is to read reviews of OTHER books in your genre and click on the names of those reviewers.

Sometimes, you'll find that those reviewers have their email address in their Amazon profile.

You can simply send them a polite email saying that you saw their review on another book similar to yours and that you'd like to send them a review copy.

I've personally gotten great reviews using this technique.

Action Item:

Make a list of 20 people that you know.

They can be friends, family, coworkers, etc.

Let them know you're launching a new book and that you'd love if they could help you by purchasing a copy at 99 cents and leaving a review.

After that, contact people that have left reviews on other books.

Keep in mind that they receive lots of solicitations, so please be respectful and understand that they're probably overwhelmed with requests.

A GREAT way to increase your chances of a response is to discuss a review that they left on a previous book.

Mention what you liked about it, how you agreed with them, or how you found it helpful.

Then you can ask if they'd be interested in learning more about your book.

Chapter 18: How to SKYROCKET Your Income and Make Long Term Profits

Now that you've launched your book and are making money, let's talk about scaling up your income.

It's very possible to start making $500 to $5000 per month from your book.

But why stop there?

First of all, businesses are built on repeat customers, so you want to build a following.

You either want to start an email list using a service like Aweber or GetResponse (I've used them both and recommend them)

Or, at the very least, you want to create a free Facebook group and invite your readers to join it.

So not only are you making money by selling the book, you're building an audience of fans that will buy from you in the future.

Other books.

Courses.

Coaching.

Anything you offer to them.

THIS is how people build real business and make job-replacing income from a tiny little book on Kindle that sells for $2.99

It's totally possible.

I've seen it happen.

I know someone that makes $10k/month selling a course.

She sells her Kindle books for 99 cents, and at the end she invites them to join her email list and her Facebook group.

Then she offers her high-ticket course.

One of my mentors wrote a book, and once it became a bestseller, offered his readers a free coaching call.

Those free coaching calls turned into $100,000 of on-going coaching packages.

All from one little book and asking his readers to join his email list.

He then used his newfound fame to write for Yahoo Finance, the Huffington Post, and get invited on a bunch of podcasts and blogs.

That's the long-term potential of having a book.

So look at your book as funnel to build a long-term business that allows you to help your customers by offering them more expensive products.

Action Item:

Invite your readers to join your Facebook group or to join your email list.

It's beyond the scope of this book to show you how to do all of this, but if you join my email list, I'll show you exactly how

(See what I did there?)

Once they follow you, give them more content, videos, articles, and tips.

They will know, like, and trust you and will be more likely to buy from you again and again, whether it's more books, software, courses, or coaching packages.

Then keep writing more books and simply repeat the process.

Conclusion

In this book, I'm shown you exactly how I created over $25,000 of passive income - with less than 15 hours of "work".

I showed you why Kindle books are such a great way to start making passive income.

I showed you how other people are making money by writing books on Amazon Kindle.

I showed you how you already are an expert and fully qualified to write a book.

And I showed you the power of creating your first bestselling book.

So now it's up to you to take action.

Imagine making $500 to $2500 per month in the next 30 days.

Imagine telling your friends and family that you wrote a bestselling book.

Imagine getting invited to speak at events, be interviewed on podcasts, and to write for large publications based on your book.

Imagine selling courses, and coaching, and consulting packages.

Imagine quitting your job and living life on your own terms.

That's all possible for you if you take **ACTION**.

So, put what you've learned to work and make it happen.

I'll Help You **TURBOCHARGE** Your Results

Don't forget to download your free bonus cheat sheet.

I want to give you a 4 page "cheat sheet" that covers the main elements in the book - so you can print it out and keep it nearby.

I show you EXACTLY how to start making $500 to $2500 per month of passive income - in the next 30 days.

Go to NOW For Your FREE Cheat Sheet

http://www.passiveincomeplaybook.com/

You'll also get exclusive bonuses, videos, and my secret resources that will help **TURBOCHARGE** your results.

I'll also invite you to join my exclusive "30 Day Challenge" where I help you generate passive income in just 30 days - for FREE.

I'll also share my top secret resources:

- The writer I use to get books written in 14 days - with no work from me
- The cover designer that I use that creates stunning covers
- How I get my books formatted for $20
- The editor/proofreader I use that charges just $1/page

So Go to NOW For All Your FREE Bonuses!

http://www.passiveincomeplaybook.com/

Please Leave a Review – It's Means a Lot

I hope you enjoyed this book. If you did, please leave me a review. It will only take 30 seconds and it would mean a LOT to me as an author.

We live and die by reviews:

- They help us know how our readers feel about our work
- They give us the motivation to keep writing
- They help others learn about our books

So please leave a review now.

Thanks in advance!